Left Wing of a Bird

Also by Arthur Vogelsang

A Planet (1983)
Twentieth Century Women (1988)
Cities and Towns (1996)

Left Wing
of a
Bird

POEMS
Arthur Vogelsang

Sarabande  Books
LOUISVILLE, KENTUCKY

No part of this book may be reproduced without written permission of the publisher. Please direct inquiries to:

Managing Editor
Sarabande Books, Inc.
2234 Dundee Road, Suite 200
Louisville, KY 40205

Library of Congress Cataloging-in-Publication Date

Vogelsang, Arthur.
     Left wing of a bird : poems / by Arthur Vogelsang.
     p.   cm.
  ISBN 1-889330-87-6 (acid-free paper) — ISBN 1-889330-88-4
(pbk. : acid-free paper)
I. Title.
PS3572.O297 L44 2003
811'.54—dc21

  2002153540

Cover image: *Left Wing of a European Roller*, 1524, Attributed to Albrecht Dürer. Pen and black ink, watercolor and gouache on parchment. 7 $\frac{7}{16}$ x 9 $\frac{7}{16}$ in. (189 x 238 mm.) Courtesy of The Woodner Collections, on deposit at The National Gallery of Art, Washington, D.C.

Cover and text design by Charles Casey Martin

Manufactured in Canada.
This book is printed on acid-free paper.

Sarabande Books is a nonprofit literary organization.

FIRST EDITION

CONTENTS

Acknowledgments   *ix*

One: Left Wing of a Bird

    Cheer Up   3

    Barnes Hill   5

    The Gods   6

    Gauguin in a Van   7

    Wrong Wrong   8

    The Writers   9

    Adults   11

    Brutal Lesson   12

    Trans Trans   13

    Round Trip 10/4–11/10   14

    Rules From a Song   15

    Defenseless in China   16

    The Red City   17

    Double Bind   18

    Thinking on My Trip West   20

    Critical   21

    Phila.   22

    It's   23

    770 MPH   25

    They Let Him Have a Rowboat   26

The Lab   27

The Line   28

Which Way?   29

A House in the Midwest   31

In Another Country   32

Ardennes Forest (Soldiers)   33

A Word in Edgewise (Sailors)   35

Bi-Coastal (Sailors of the Air)   36

Re Who   38

Folk Song   39

Almost Indigent   40

Hamnet   41

Two: Come to Your Senses

Flowers on a Beach   45

Liquids in Quantities   48

Graves in Johnson County   50

Instructions to the Alien   58

Three   60

The Writers 2   62

Three: Right Wing of a Bird

After   65

Carolinas   66

Baltimore   68

Archive on Ice (After the Act, Pig on the Ice)   70

Words in Your Mouth   73

Gone   74

The *Iliad,* the *Odyssey,* and *Heart of Darkness*   76

The Author   *78*

ACKNOWLEDGMENTS

Some of the poems appeared previously, a few in different form, in the following publications. Thanks to their editors.

"770 MPH" and "Which Way?" in *Crazyhorse*. "Double Bind" and "Flowers on a Beach" in *The Colorado Review*. "Critical," "The Lab," and "Liquids in Quantities" in *Denver Quarterly*. "Ardennes Forest (Soldiers)," "A Word in Edgewise (Sailors)," "Bi-Coastal (Sailors of the Air)," "Defenseless in China," "Gauguin in a Van," "The *Iliad*, the *Odyssey*, and *Heart of Darkness*," "Tattoo," and "They Let Him Have a Rowboat" in *Interim*. "The Line," "Liquids in Quantities," and "Which Way?" in *The New Bread Loaf Anthology of Contemporary Poetry*. "In Another Country" and "The Red City" in *River City*. "Graves in Johnson County" in *Volt*.

One

Left Wing of a Bird

Cheer Up

I used to enjoy sleeping so much
But now I'm cold to the bone
Or dreaming too much.
The extra dreams unsettling, gross,
Or both.
Then there's the day—
There's no place to be—bed, woods,
I'm tired in the woods and afraid I can't run when I can.
Or along the river in the park
Nothing is apt
Where the path stops and you must walk
And you have to cover your legs—
I can't go out there too far.
I really don't want to nod off anymore.
It's quiet at night, too quiet, too quiet to sleep.
Something coming from *everywhere*, mocking me, no,
Mocking just my sleep, driving me back to dream.

"Where you crumple like paper in two hands
Then lie whole and unconscious.
I lie an hour unconnected to either world.
I remember anything. Nothing is apt.
Right now remember the Hopis? lived
With opened doors, no doors, to connect
With anything when they were sleeping,
No vulnerability unless

A room or apartment was closed
And they were *trapped by the foot like animals.*
They lived high in the air,
Took up ladders.
They joined the everything.
Or not exactly. In winter, erected doors.
Chilly airless rooms, but not cold,
And wrapped around each other.
Their dreams came like trains which didn't exist
Or waves they had never seen."

Barnes Hill

Fog but bright
And the king's mistress wants to hold hands
But they may not. She wants
An eclipse of the sun,
As in Spain,
But is misguided about the thin dark
As if it could be utter blackness.
If he would hold hands in the darkness
She would fuck him for two or three minutes.
As it happens
There is an eclipse in the fog.
It is not dark.
It is darker but exhilarating,
Nearly euphoric, not euphoric, and, like that,
Bright fog, nice thin dark.
The king understands a public show of affection.
He does not think human emotions are much of a mystery.
A flock of birds turns abruptly,
Lower than the hill the group has climbed.
The birds are afraid, he knows,
As he knows for sure the eclipse is benign
But he does not know why.

The Gods

Strong strange behavior and strange strong events
He could disappear she could fly
And they did and it thundered too much
A dove with a chain
Hooked a knight
Not outdone a swan pulled a boat
And "slept" with a thin princess
Actually they slept all night
After muscular staccato coitus...
Versus simpler pleasures and steady pain
Gods and their activities are a beautiful artifice
Like a magnifying glass or harmony
Or a successful check-forging scheme
Or letters intercepted to change my opinion of you
I'd like to know a secret and have wealth at the same time
Not separately and I don't want to work for it
If I could I'd swell that grasshopper big enough
For me to ride through the city...
I'd tell everybody, He's okay, he doesn't bite.

Gauguin in a Van

All babies' fins, and all their tails, grow.
How fine you look in a dress, Deirdre, in Kentucky,
South of here, among unformed faces and unformed hills.

Why would you think photos of the foetus
Would change the mind of Emily Dickinson
Any more than they have changed ours? Go.

Ditto an encounter with an engorged penis.
The mood would, of course, be the entire case.
North of here, in chilly summer, in rain.

Deirdre and Emily in the rain are pregnant.
They shop for food, they urinate, they have hope,
Hanging out in a big Swedish station wagon.

Let me go home.
It was a mistake to bless me as you have.
My fate is gentle with many flares along the side of the road.

Wrong Wrong

The lie at the bottom of the attack against men
Isn't an evil lie, for women are not evil,
(Men are) but it's a lie of omission.
Most of the great poetry, most of the good poetry
(Novels and plays too) has been written by men.
I don't know if that's the truth or not.
But women won't tell you—never, never—
That the bottom of the lyric impulse (and the dramatic
Which is an impulse they really hate)
Is sex and romantic love which men have huge bags
Of compared to women (also in our organization—
I mean our whole organized life—women aren't allowed to be
Full persons) and so if the romantic myth and the desire
And the muscles to make an epiphany or a rapture
Is mostly on the one side, well, I wouldn't talk about it
Much either, if I was one of them. That'd be just a white lie.

By dusk ships on our screen,
Bodies maimed in Asia Minor,
And at night a break back to regular shows—
In the morning paper clutched two Homo sapiens
And two stone picture journals
Of sexual tableaux with scripted screaming—
Lucky me, I have become hardened, like a doll fashioned from scars,
To almost everything,
So I'm sure my idea must be a dream and the filthiest lie.

The Writers

Loco rolling with a motive
To St. Louis out of the snow

To a plane fast as the sound
Of your voice asking for water

Which ignites a dream like engines coughing
But spun and fluent

But loose on ice—careening—dream you row
Warm with crippled men

On shallow water to an island
Where, tidal mud, their twang,

They ask ma'am who are you
And where do you come from?

"…While we are flying, as if captured together,
Did you know in my torn burnt book

There was a quarrel, shocking in its bitterness
To the narrator who was also the prize? Me.

In the great hall with the twisting stair
My suitor and I slept, but apart. That's OK,

But what's troubling—he did not seem like you—
But like a guest the same size—a red-haired

Crazy person from that inner island I rowed to in your dream
Or like a brother my shape and size.

On the train my thighs, my hair fixed for my suit,
Seemed separate from me

As if hanging in a butcher's shop
Or in a Native American window in New York.

Plane, nothing to read in the rain on the window.
Train, nothing can form in the massively falling snow...."

Adults

As we went cursing and driving through Delaware,
The southern part where cursing in cars was forbidden,
In search of the local tomato, and only it,
We got very tired, we got very hungry,
And we yelled to each other feed me.
An actual real general store under the corn
Had hearts beside the pulsing fish,
Homemade heart sandwiches, and the mom and pop
Thought your wife and I were related,
To be specific thought I was the husband,
And hated us, and liked you.
And your blessing of each item, each,
As homemade, even the tiny blades for small saws
And the box of straight pins open above the popcorn.
"Do you have any wigs made in Pennsylvania?" we asked,
And felt immediately awful for you, I think,
Though she was gasping and wanted more.
The two of you were so tired and heavy
I had to drive her peculiar car and curse out the window
For all three, searching for gears
On the steep up-curve of that monstrous bridge,
And more gears down, specifically second
And its merciful grip and indiscriminate love
Of its own metal and us.

Brutal Lesson

Whether what he remembered was bent to the chew and digest of
    his line,
Or was true like a photo, or an aerial photo, or a TV show
About it, was not his problem. His mother painted from life
Or from memory, it didn't matter. It came out like Hopper
Or the Big Bopper and that was fine. This is an apple, he could say,
Yeah, and after you eat it, it *was* an apple, dig? Dig
Is what we said in the fifties in Philadelphia or California like alors
In Paris or dig in Paris, like cocksucker at the bus station
Where I actually worked, bless *me*. He advised, when you get into
    the big scenes
You don't select objective correlatives, you just get your head right
And put in everything in that voice that blesses everything
Which is why it's easy, really, and you don't have to remember
    anything,
Or memory is a veil, simple enough, but memory is never a gauze
    stage curtain
From behind which figures walk, embed themselves,
Do a show on the thick threads,
And then walk toward us, who said that?

Trans Trans

They were the gentlest, the mountain ranges,
Small and beautiful one of them,
And the other was very very high but gentle.
Holding books in a car, distracted by my chatter
Of a way range to range in rush hour,
She much wanted to tear into the books at her leisure.
I would drive away. If I drove away
She would come too, wouldn't she have to?
I've said before, the policemen were helpless
And torn and sick because they could not help
The woman being abused, they were undercover.
In our other lives we are abused by a tone. It hurts,
Maybe not that much,
But boy it hurts a lot I must say.
Knights at beige desks, ladies in the moat
Embracing thugs who are ragged, wet, half-naked;
They also demand quarters. I would swim away.

Round Trip 10/4–11/10

Summer horses have not disappeared
Into an adobe's open door
Or out
Winds of whoopie at night
Leather clouds today
A pre-night grin at the crossing gate
The flag and a book in her hand
As if we were soldiers not sleepers

But coming back in November
Winter horses
In a crossing by night
Will have walked to the track and away
Hoofs will have printed in the thin snow
The woman with them or not
Escaped or not
I will see from the huge aluminum train

Rules From a Song

It is a crow and not a cow that watches you in the highlands of
New Mexico.
It is numbers of Arabian mathematicians that fling
The bridge over the Chesapeake
And not big muscles
Of gorgeous workers in love with their families, which may not fling
Asphalt. Math bends steel over the Delaware. It may fling.
The crow is hideous, I love him so much,
Ounce for ounce he is the most powerful animal
And eats bugs to exhaustion.
Detroit is north of Canada.
Lies are bred in the tidal pond of the family drama. Across it
Children jump short, splash, and laugh uncontrollably, rolling
toward the sea.
Nothing may be built over the sea. A human heart is for sale,
Ten thousand dollars at the drop of a hat, and a ticket to ride.

Defenseless in China

I am an American not a German,
Defenseless in China
On a riverbank.

One minute. You,
Change your clothes, please would you,
Impersonate in the fog...hair too...in town...

There was threatening music
In the movies, perverse during snacks
Before the movie began. Figure.

It was one of those relationships we
Could change our clothes together.
There were farmers with oxen and hand plows

Across the water. Plane tickets,
Snow at night on the edge of spring,
Blonds, strawberry and ash.

The Red City

The glue fell out of the book, 1801.
She said in the book,
"I carved a tiny pumpkin for Halloween 2001."
A sound remains over 200 years, choking of course.
Or there's no sound, there's a Polaroid:
An eyedropper towers above a squash.
Tinfoil is spread in front of its face—
To make it blush more she says
Than the little piece of cut candle inside can.

Or it was a whim in 1801 to celebrate a couple of centuries,
To just flat out do something for 2001,
So far away, so science fiction.
How many grandmothers ago, five? six?
A cousin is dead, to the south, in the Cleveland National Forest,
The last of the clan, except for one,
Who has carved a pumpkin in 1801
Or a tiny one for Halloween 2001,
Warm yellow meat, odor of fresh glue.

Double Bind

You are her but you are like me.
What's the sun got that the moon hasn't got?

Tell me a cowboy stood on the sun.
She told me a cowboy stood on the moon.

Huge, I am one of these, rotating, ochre,
Said to have a skin as the earth has a skin.

When the moon was in the blue sky
While over there the sun,

On my skin pigs, sheep, and chickens
Ran feral as all the people died,

The horror of a chicken herd in a deserted playground.
Did that happen to you too?

And she is a piano dawdler like you.
You two fit on the stool like twins

And I fit there too, poking at pieces for three.
You are like me so stop.

OK, I guess I'd better watch out. I could become
A flatbed truck hauling two pianos

Under the moon in the blue sky
And over there the sun.

Thinking on My Trip West

Happy days were the fingers
Of a powerful cloudy madman
That held down the water to you
As you drove like a man.

He would never admit flying-fear
Never never and said he'd pilot
He'd love to pilot a jerkwater
Plane with in it
A small dark exquisitely sexy teenager.

It's so like a song darling he'd say to
You, shit if it ain't
And shit if it ain't Gallup
Imagine the hunks of beef and the
Strange vegetables and all that shitty food
These Indians in dire need of help eat
And would feed us in that cafe.

Secret mountains and snide valleys—
Where up so high poking a finger through a gray cloud
Someone explains, "The blank life
Dangling down into the purple bloody valleys,"
Such as the one from Ohio to New Mexico,
"Is my life though I'm beautiful and full."

Critical

Life star, dirt
Is your baby,
More valuable than snow
(Shine on each without my command).
Long books in strong buildings,
Thin summary books in the gorgeous postperson's hands.
They are true, crystallize truly
Or separate into the benign bottles of chapters
What is one, or badly named, or before people.
This morning something red and powerful
Sent to me, me personally, me
The center of all blue suns,
Is handed over by an untouchable young black woman
—Bad Kafka Critique at the front door
Enigmatic forever or until most people become like him.

Phila.

A lunatic tried to hail a cab
And you for whom a poet's wife
Has washed many a time his come-filled rag, you
Moved to help so the dirty prophet turned
As if speaking to you at dinner and said,

Nothing ever happened
Napoleon an idea
Patterns in the mud
I stepped out of my
Puzzled shadow.

We have pieced it together.
When you go, I want to become something literal
Like a horse on the baby-blue Walt Whitman bridge.

It's

You'll pass many trees
In its palm a hand shall hold a reflective lake
So some more trees will be easy to see
And in the usual way when you walk
On your lawn you'll pass seven trees
You'll pass many trees
They are in houses and
We do not go to deserts
Only senior professors of creosote
Are treeless where the low blue bushes
Are low and blue and sharp in the sharp sand
You'll pass many trees
Professors of ice are treeless in Greenland
But not you you'll pass many trees
Not on the water
How many sixths of the earth is water
Five and the sixth is water changing into saplings
Or do you mean saplings becoming water
But you know for sure remember
You have passed many trees and
You will pass many trees
In the mall thousands
In the mountains more
The universe is empty yes
Or the universe is packed full yes
One or the other foolish to take a middle position

The trees use the wind to be the trees
Or the wind uses the trees to be the wind
Like no darkness possible without light
And boy, for sure, vice versa
No light without d
You'll pass many trees

770 MPH

Sometimes the bad President ate anything that moved
Away from the shot
Then was overtaken, shattered.
Near a restaurant
Lugubrious grass grows over
The edge of a bank.
Steep the bank. Hidden the stream.
Distantly to the duck or the snake
An orange amoeba appeared
Followed by the steel-jacketed lead.
In the time
Frame of the animal it acted and moved in front of the shot.
The lead approached,
And it made tracks.

They Let Him Have a Rowboat

There was dirty work to be undone.
Behind the sun
Overdressed stewardesses,
High propeller-driven planes
Drone overhead, seen.
Where? Behind the pink cloud
In the weak light to the left of the sun.
Dirty work has been done
Beyond the boat's range,
In the blue in the green strange
Spasm of bulk of water
Beyond the lees
Wherein I kept a cautious place,
Hairy tan rope cut and sinking in the deep green
Water, dirty work was done.

The Lab

He stood. "Agitation," he said,
In a sonorous commanding voice,
"Trembling, shimmering, i.e., fear."
Much of it filled a tub
Like four hundred iron balls and some water
Mass of pain
Individual round items
Searing iron balls
Each with riders
Quivering in the saddle
Tough tiny riders
Of that size that's just visible
Where they rode seemed to them flat, unrelieved
Eastern Colorado facing east
Tune of my hand
The prongs of the fingers hum
And the hand wanders in panic
As a rowboat on the Pacific will always bounce and shiver
Bolts and wood

The Line

What am I, suppose I am,
A cliff of flowers grabbed and shook
Like a large light blanket across a bed
Across a beach and into the Pacific Ocean?
Like a lure such tall flowers
Are arranged on a steel hook curving a half mile.
What is the motion of the blanket,
Creases chasing waves
In the interior air of the bedroom? The shaft
Of the hook is a sandy road one mile long
With oyster shells and crows,
Big lean ones, blue-black and afraid,
Fleeing over the hairy yellow flowers.
The black animals fly inland over two fields
Where there will be a house of ballet
In the future. It is a place of hints and rain
Now, like whispers during a slight slap of flesh.
Other birds were like birds
Free in a house which fly excitedly
But always near the humans.
Though he's on one stage,
A dancer is making brief perches
In other rooms, you said, and that's most like you.
Our doors an hour from the water, inland.

Which Way?

We dreamed as we swam.
The surf was a radio fading off its signal.
In the back of our minds and in back of us
Were naked bathers,
Each one big as a palm on a small thin beach.
Wet Paris and wet Africa
Filled each bather's mind.

We thought as we swam
That we did not need our brains,
That we would not use them.
It was our desire.
We would float, in our ardent wish.
The universe was out to sea.
Crazy to believe it had an end.
It was limitless, of course,
A concept that solved a lot,
And all were insane who had a metaphor for it.

We would float and pretend
A limb would flake off
And dissolve into grains before it hit bottom.

Our bodies of blood,
In the entire universe one other liquid like it,
Which was the water in which we swam.

Someone must have been on the inland road
Staring at the bathers on the beach.
It would be tempting.
Most of the time they were the normal size
Of ripe older teenagers nude on a beach.

Beyond the inland road was all existence.
Pianos, bananas, printing presses, aspirin.
Our desire to float conscious as salt
Was as good a reason as any to turn and swim
And swim and swim.

A House in the Midwest

Voices may come from another room
But when they do not and there is someone there
How do we know, or are we wrong?
How may it be we who are there? We
Are here. The cats
As if they knew what we know
But gave it no importance, come here
And look. How about something? they say,
Anything? The ghosts, if there are any
On the whole plain, must be waiting
Like the vase of flowers in there,
Colorful, half alive, many little colored suns
Harmless like beasts longing to stare at us.

In Another Country

Driven back into a territory of red fur coats
And forests of short knarled pepper trees
Growing into a shallow ocean,
The man and the woman considered changing their first names.
Their first names were almost the same
And that could be a taboo, there, as here.
They owned one red dish, among many, and used it often.
One owned a red shirt that was often worn inside out
By mistake, like a warning of falsely crying wolf.
They came up on an empty elevated freeway, empty.
As when the ocean disappears for a half mile
Just before a rogue wave
Disintegrates an entire town of four thousand
Flat to the sand? Yes, like that. Where *behind* them
Five motorcycle cops slowed to a halt the five lanes
And a highway worker in a red vest hustled across the lanes
Picking up shattered stuff that looked like flesh but was rubber.
All this was true, but the part about the names.
What I will say is taboo.
No, their names were not Nicky and Nicole, no, no.
Even if they knew red was a warning, which *was* true,
There was nothing to do until red seemed more than red.

Ardennes Forest (Soldiers)

A bite
In the back of the thigh.
Many such pink steel scars...
Some have them...some don't.
Pieces of tin sprayed as clouds spray water.
A film and a book
About a vicious, tribal society,
Gangsters or anachronistic mountain rebels,
A second reading, a viewing, another reading...
I watched in a way that slowed...
I read word for word
And understood
Everyone, everything,
Was like that,
The smile a feint,
The handshake a unique secret signal,
The hairy sexual organs
Seeking proper angles,
And very beautiful today
No matter how they had seemed,
So for a little while ecstasy
Like a paper plane tossed,
The child stung as if a mosquito...
Surprise, reality, better
Than the inviolable body...
From a welt at a great distance,

Near the knees or the neck,
Around the groin,
Pain, peace, not overwhelming as rain may not be.

A Word in Edgewise (Sailors)

Gist: An encounter with a rogue wave
On a shore near a marina.

Ran as fast as his legs could obey a bitter unusual fear
While impressed with the giant thing
In the way after a first trip to the sun
The sun is much bigger than promised
So beyond the bounds of what anything should be
As to be unfair and firing hydrogen bombs.

Word for word:
This story joined his repertoire.

It was an attempt to describe size
Not a story! Shithole! Attempt...! Size...!
As he escaped injury and stayed dry
He went at the impossible task more and more
Until finally the speech grew on one
Unscientific repetitious no ending
Now I must have a wave like that after me
Not on demand
An accident not waiting to happen
Not god-driven, fate a weak tea, and not at sea.

Bi-Coastal (Sailors of the Air)

Worse shadows in September,
What did you think,
Black in kitchens
Or where there had been a river.

Brassy horns over dialogue.
Advice,
As if there were an issue,
Like, Breathe normally.

Meanwhile, don't deny it, there's
An oar, hear
The oars on a bay!?
I wish I was tired in a friendly space.

Men on horses were lost in the mountains west of Baltimore.
Help them.
Afraid in a car in a desert
I advise:

Breathe normally folks
Breathe normally son
Breathe normally you all.

The surface of machines in orbit is tan
Or nearly silver like burnished vaseline.

Not sure if sex is a fuel
Or people are an illusion
Or men are simply more rapacious toward their prey
Than women, possibly it is vice versa, but I must say,

Ma'am, I wish you were a terrific extemporaneous speaker,
I wish you were forty-three.
If I could express all my wishes
Without fear of punishment,

And since I can,
As we will not return from here,
Why do I not?

There are shadows in August
And worse ones in September,
Black in arroyos and in kitchens.

In the river bottom, fuck! fine cool
Sand so far from the sea
Time's not up but it will be.

Re Who

She says good-bye in each conversation
Like it was a manifesto
Spoken above centrifugal soup—pieces stirred
Like pieces of moon, melting rocks, and Uranus never still;
They bump and are speared with a fork.
It is not a clear, limpid soup.
It is not a Barnum and Bailey world though
The voice of a toy is accurate expression, repeatable
At dusk in the face of the voices of bugs.
Is "tremendously hard of hearing" an error
Or an emphasis? Why is "centrifugal"
Condemning to one who speaks alertly?
What a prodigious pot! Still,
If suns are carrots and the hot ones are,
Elongated, orange, with some green leaves,
And our ships are celery with some green leaves
And teflon troughs for strolling in space or cheese,
And our potatoes are dirty and hilly like planets, well, so,
There is no pot, there is no end, no shape, no nothin',
And such insistent prediction of death
Is a rider swallowing steel on a white horse, standing,
You've seen 'em.

Folk Song

We may not meet on the other side.
We will be unconscious, you idiot.
We will be...nothing...what do I
Mean by nothing? Far from the stench
And shred flesh of our wounds, as far from it as
We are now when we smell like peaches,
And run, and go to movies with a flexible eye.
As for whether there is an other side,
I can not now say,
Or rather, I will not say, it is too
Final, it is too unlike anything,
I do not want to say it to you if I could.

Almost Indigent

Where to eat, where to play the piano,
Where to play blackjack, where to sleep,
What bells in the river
That is a harbor too?
Where are feral animals to be saved?

Under the only bush.
Bells have crooned on buoys in the rain.
Today they are a stark sound in the sun,
In your bed,
At your table,
Where there is a big free piano at the school
The other way, across the small, foul river.

Hamnet

Her twin brother
Was nevertheless living
And would return to us.
A magician, raising each assistant from a chair,
Says there they are.

A brain twister in a car,
To waste the time, for children
A twister of facts
With an inevitable answer
If you took the road

With three rocks to the left
At its beginning and end
Like a jetty's scab on the scar of the jetty.
In the future, there, the mocking chairs
Of a completely empty audience.

Of the twins born in 1585
The one of our title died
At eleven, Shakespeare's son.
Judith lived.
Imagine if you were twenty-seven

And fell into a nap
And woke near decay

As I am, well,
That's how it is, since you asked,
And understand, and are living.

Speaking to you is no problem.
Language as a conundrum, that's a game in a dream.
Childhood romantic love and sex, that's
Lovely and character-building between children,
A fantasy like levitation.

Two

Come to Your Senses

Flowers on a Beach

Here's my thoughts.
You know my heart
By radio phone
Postcard
Scream
Mobile phone
Scratch pad
Whisper
And conversations in automobiles,
In dining rooms,
And on porches and all of these are different
From conversations on the regular telephone.
The waves are terrible, their noise is like bombs,
And they are too big for the ocean.
I wish I wasn't here,
That there were no thoughts,
And that everything took place in my heart
In those manifold forms
Of communication,
The scratch pad
The radio phone
The porch.
Often we talked about meat or hatred.
It may be that we did not have value systems
Or they were embedded.
Standing in the water of my pool

For we have fled from the beach
In the sick heat of the middle afternoon,
Standing with two polar poets,
An odd combination of rare and burnt,
We were speaking of two women poets
Who stood in the same water last week.
As in a photograph by someone serious fooling around,
Imagine the chests of us, the three men,
Inappropriately emphasized
Like uncooked chicken on a plate of water.

None of my students she said spreading
Just one of her legs in the deep water
Understands how the white male is becoming a victim
Rather than the central hero
Of an intercontinental tragedy
But I do. I'm trying to fix this for you.
I'll tell you when I'm ready
To talk about that other thing.

To forces beyond us if there are any
The cut bunch
Is the same as people standing in water
With heads like flowers—
The wetness where the stems are cut
Is nothing
Or it is…it is…
But more likely everything is the same—
Amputation's rudeness, pretty flowers—
Though standing in the pool is quieter

Than standing neck-deep in the ocean
And there is less motion
While adults weeping in the surf
Is like...like...adults weeping in the surf.

They are stems;
The waves are flowers on them, big for them.
If one of them dives, she, he, is a stem
And the whole ocean is the flower.
Then, as everywhere where there is no up and down,
They are leaking stems trying to root in the sky.
Baby if it is any consolation the soul makes pictures
Efficiently to the end as well as at birth or as a wily adult
And they are its utterance it has no other.

Liquids in Quantities

Not twice a day but half a time or once, a tide
On the sun is a tide. In the hideous person Jackson Pollock's brain
About that frequently a bay of enzymes or a gulf of sea water
Or a sea of pee receded on a beach
And of course bulged on another beach being a tide or
On another day a joke with no punch line but a nice middle
Brought a minor smile to his face as when the sun smiles.
If you don't think the sun smiles, look at the moon would you
And deny the infectious planetary humor,
One big ochre organ setting off spasms in the liquid or the dust of
    the other
That lasts a day or a half-day or a day-and-a-half.

When another massive body calls to the sun come
Its incandescent sauce shifts like our salty water.
There is actually a bulge in the water off Delaware
When there is actually a concavity or long shallow crater in it off
    Spain.
Places on the sun are not places
Due to so many places there being purple gas
That changes to disappearing dry white relish
Like a surf of only pebbles and no water
Or that explodes as if it were its job
Which it is to explode as much as possible.
All the words on the sun are for explosion.
You could think of a sun joke like over there is the Sea of Ruth

But it would never smile because as soon as you said "over" it
would explode.
How may it have tides? then and how may those tides
Be approximately like something that went on in Jackson's dreadful
brain?
Settle this first: as the sun is one of a kind around here
It smiles to itself alone so it doesn't need a punch line, yes?
A man in the street would say that's OK, let it do it, yes?
A woman about whom many have said what an eminently just
piece of work that gorgeous
Little weasel is if asked in the street with her mind on her next trial
Would say "it is fine for the sun to laugh or even explode
At something with no demonstrably absurd point."
I said to the moon which would not answer
I said to it as it thought of the answer to another question
Suppose tides on the sun
Is just a shot at a beautiful idea or something which is like something
And not really boiling methane that's a big surf,
And if the sun actually saw on itself waves like that it would
explode them
But the one appearance would be the beginning of the end what do
you think?
The moon called to the Atlantic and to the Pacific by turning like
the moon.

Graves in Johnson County

Want to try to get home
Without a funny thing
Happening on the way?
Me I just ran into
An anthropological stunner:
More people alive
Than all the dead put together.
Ha-ha-ha, ha-ha-ha.

Who would put the dead together?
Hee-hee-hee.
A person back home, back east,
Like an animal
Sees others
As part of the food chain,
Walking meat
To become him,
His chest,
His soul, which he has,
Which is like a city's humidity.
The phrase vaporized meat
In one of my poems.
Dig?

Thank you for your applause.
Most of our fun here,

Three others and me,
Is reading what's chiseled.
Death year, badly put message.
Birth year, wow!
The field of cut white stones
Is a trap without a lock,
Like memory,
The only supernatural thing.
Wait till you get a load of my machine
To compare memory,
Five- or nine-sided recollections,
Device of steadily melting iron
And purloined cartilage,
Of no use,
No practical use,
Brain fruit clustered
Like rounded monuments
To you to you to you.

Thank you.
One of those three
Has a personal taboo on me.
Wait a minute, thank you.
Ladies and germs. Huh huh huh. All right,
I know it rhymes.
All right. Just a minute now. As I was saying,
She has a taboo on me,
So probably I was not included,
Tell me if you think I was,
In an embrace

Among the small markers
Over and down a hill
That's a ripple
Because the glaciers
Pushed and stopped.
Just so the embrace
Could be hidden
From the other two people,
Just so the embrace
Could occur at all—
The glacier did its work
And withdrew.
What counts is what I say,
Where I say it.
Meanwhile, the way she says it.

A portrait. However,
In the car
Plans for dinner disintegrated.
There were two women
And another guy,
Three yous
As Merle Brown said there should be,
And me.
The question marks that abounded
Were benign, still are,
As in a social history
Safe from kissing.
Among the discussions
Of vapor,

Mores in wagons,
And infancy,
The car went on.

It had done so.
Dinner had disintegrated
In the graveyard.
Will you believe me, a happy place,
Many question marks,
Benign and many, there.
Because the car had gone on,
Because the glacier's
Entire purpose
Was to hide
The briefest affair
Under a hill,
An encounter so brief
There probably was no kiss,
But the glacier's entire purpose
Was to hide the embrace
From the other two people,
For only those specific reasons
I need each of your kinds of memory,
You your honesty
That might admit
Some or no feeling for me,
You your tendency
To fabricate first
And outright lie second,
You your flexibility

And elegance
With stories about eating,
Molestation,
And unrelieved pain.
May I have these
In three letters please?

In a play,
Which is a trap with a lock,
This would be called
Begging a something or other.
Asking for the machine
Would be too,
And if God allowed
Or the desperate playwright opted
The machine to appear and work,

This would be seen
By even the weakest of audiences
As a deus ex machina.
Ooo-hee-hee and excuse me.
All graves are a deus ex machina.
All graves are failures as such.
They are like radios
Made before electricity.
Thank you for your applause.
I was the driver.
That was the second of my portraits.

Marriage is a business.
You will have enemies
Who leave you alone now.
You will be like a two-personed statue
Versus a rock.
The insane hate the rocks.
The well hate the statue, or, sorry,
The well may and might hate the statue.
But in the contract, the bond,
There is a power
Like an alligator's peculiar muscles,
Easy to hand-open the jaws
But irresistible force squeezing closed.
If we did that,
We'd have to move
To Shingle Point
In the Northern Yukon,
We'd have to flush
Baby alligators
Down the toilet
And dig in the ice
Or freeze the human bodies
Until the summer
And its persistent day.
Arthur grasped the story
Of the county's lost campaign
Against the Rodin piece
On the rich lovers' mausoleum

Depicting a dedicated act of intercourse,
Since stolen of course.
Of course of course.

I brought you here
To listen to my routine,
To try myself to fall in love
Or secondarily to get laid,
And to introduce you to each other.
There are no various versions to compare
And your presence,
Though only a rhetorical one,
Not like really being together
In a car or in a graveyard,
Has been terrific
For two days of writing
And I admit
We are all whirling balls
Of self-interest as are our sun or our earth which by gravity
Pull in hard and mush up what's without heat shield or parachute
So it becomes them
And so I have made you into me
But while it's now
Would you look around
At the field of stones
And answer my question?

Encore

This is not a tradition in stand-up.
What am I supposed to do,
Come back out and say OK get this, listen up, here's one more joke?
Shakespeare didn't say to himself
Now I'll sit down and write *Hamlet*,
He was, you know, in a process when he did it
And my stuff's like that rather than one-liners.
I can't dance and I can't sing
So I became a poet;
I suppose I could ask the orchestra
If they knew any poem and then try to sing along with them,
    whatever it was.
Let me ask you instead am I slipping away
Like ice mistakenly let go on downhill ice?
Are you?

Instructions to the Alien

If we want to read about it, kisses
Are more interesting than ———
If the characters are well-rounded
And there is an historical imperative,
Oddly enough. If we don't want to read,
It is by far more exciting to ———.

Or a journey in a car, har har,
Would not be a journey
To those in the 18th century,
It'd be more like moving along
Fast in a small nice room
And the smooth concrete bumps would be like itches.

You've said what's kept you away
Is that when we line up all our options
And the best one is obvious
To any sentient being, even a ——— dog,
We often choose the painful messy one
And we *know* we do,

For instance this has been called the imp
Of the perverse by Edgar Allan Poe,
And tragedy by Aristotle.
Our books with transubstantiation

In them are a minor genre, even though you
Swear by it and go a long way in it

And are here, from using it. I don't
Really want to get into killing and love,
Those acts isolated and per se,
Just so you can begin reading history.
Stick with novels and poetry
And the fact that each one of us is all

The characters in our dreams, no one else
Is in them. Two hundred years is a long time;
Ancestors may not be here and we may not be there,
And there were and are journeys,
Which are different than wishes.
I've told you—you wish, you do,

We wish, we fantasize. That's why
There's novels and poetry, and kisses
In them. Kisses are a cult when they are the end
All and be all; I tried this by myself
For a while and needed help of the sort
I'm about to explain. Help me.

Three

By other animals an animal—run into a canyon—
With no way out.
Like too much blood in a drinking glass
Filled from a slow endless tube
That will not stop,
Its anger fills it and it is free.
We are sad, we are the sad ones.
We think it has abandoned hope
And we pin our precious selves on it,
But it doesn't have any self.
It hates completely
(More than completely—remember the overflowing glass?)
And has many times its own strength
When its spine is shredded
Or its legs are eaten first
By others—careless and joyful—in their own euphoria.

———————

"What she knows about medicine and the human body
You could put under your fingernail.
I got her on to my doctor"
(Where is he going with this?)
"And she did stuff like take half the dose or drink coffee.
She used to call me up every other day
But now she's thinking of committing herself

And talks less and less to everybody.
My guy's an internist and I don't think he can help her anymore.
The thing is, we've got to work hard at helping each other
And never stop, or else what's the point, so I think
You should call her, it would do her some good.
Of course I know there isn't any point ever,
But c'mon."

———

Cannot be reached, our high fence, their thick wall,
Choked out our open window
Strangled by a dog as we're in bed
A raccoon with its big claws and hands
Gets the air but the air becomes a fallen accordion
Again—again—five minutes—
Through punctures in its windpipe,
(See them the next day)
Now in breaking bushes in the dark, *opposite* the bed, a high fence
And a thick wall and cannot be reached.
The dog is a good-looking sheepherder that can be petted;
We can see nothing, we remember him.
Our neighbors have a high wall, won't answer the phone.
There is enough time for us to call (as much time as we want)
As the strong dog exerts himself at his work.

The Writers 2

One, a Native American student of mine is like you or me.
He says, I'm not sure I would eat (if I had my choice now)
Some of my enemies; frequently I'd scalp them,
But not always, I guess.
What I'd really like to do is flee in a boat,
Whenever I want, as a solution to anything.
How may I cluster turning points in my book
If there are none in my life, he asks me.

The second thing honey is you and what you know,
The five building blocks of *The Great Gatsby*
And the two separate mad halves of *Full Metal Jacket*.
You say, the cities of the East Coast are in a great forest.
You say to me, if you think a ten-year arc put into a three-day arc
Is anything anybody in their right mind would believe,
You are a special asshole.

This is the way it went,
Week after week. Experience was not assigned meaning.
Hunger and penetration were driving forces that led to the ocean,
Imagine that, insane lucky journeys in wooden boats
That led to this, and for what? Finally this is this,
As shy smiles on the faces of the infected will tell you.

Three

Right Wing of a Bird

After

"...the deer-poaching legend bore strange fruits of romantic elaboration." —S. Schoenbaum

Gertrude Stein in armor in a tree, patiently waiting for a deer to walk below. Not for food will Stein jump. Has a butcher's knife. Thinks life is tough and flat opposed to art, that waiting has no dramatic shape. Waiting is very different from everything, she may think. So she may stay, ready to leap each second with armor intact, the suit has been designed so she may pee, an opening. Is it female armor then, liar? It is male armor, modified so she may solo, self-sufficiently in the woods, and to imitate Shakesp., so she may say she did it alone. So she says so, to imitate Shakes. in his lost years, the poacher. Fresh activity, totally without her companion. After two hours, have to go, have to. Is the deer a dope? Can the deer not super smell? A puddle? Has it happened out of a tree? Probably. A beast of prey is not an artist, for these moments I am not an artist, she may say. Not hungry, she is patient in a tree. It is a silver suit of armor and the knife is one piece.

Gravity will call her down to the deer. The weight on the animal's back will crumple its middle to the ground for a second. Stein will miss her one stroke, clanging the blade safely into the thigh plate of the bright armor. She will think, but has not thought yet, I am divested of correlation. The animal neither expects nor understands pity. The weight, gravity's valentine, pushes its middle to the ground, briefly, and it is not hurt as we shall see. Back with its herd, the legend of the strange fruit needed no elaboration. It was accessible to mule deer, Chinese river deer, white-tailed deer, pere David's deer, all, and was a story with a broad range of concerns, including the astounding patience of Stein. The animal rises and runs.

Carolinas

*"Nor have I seen
More that I may call men than you..."*
—The Tempest

Charles Olson, a big man, has altered. His fins were once his arms. Otherwise the same, same addresses, students, toothbrush, shoes, head. Same *Moby-Dick* research. Same poem In Cold Hell, with the line ya, selva oscura, but hell now, not altered.

Charles Olson, a big man, has added a kidnapping to his biography. An addition, nothing altered. All biographies have the same ending. Autobiographies may not have an ending, by their nature. Did you ever try to write when you were dead?

Charles Olson has successfully captured a person. Dangerous moonlight was whitening the turf (Alice Fairfax-Lucy in S. Schoenbaum) where she waded. The turf was the largest tide on earth, which was ebbed and low, low. Charles ran from the thick forest of the island, which grew to the beach. He did not run like the girl he captured or like a big man, he ran gracefully and lifted her up. They continued into the whitening surf for what seemed an interminable time. Because of the length of the tide, he ran for one minute, then had to walk in white boil for a couple minutes before he swam.

If there is no indication in his life story of the characteristics of the female he kidnapped, she *may have been* a powerful swimmer. She was at least 15 yr and no older than 28.

Arduous the search for her characteristics in his bio. As if gauze like the thinnest summer blanket were laid over them on the beach they slept. As if audience by whim or vote could frequently change Charles' fins and arms according to the challenge facing him, she participated in his life away from the island and gave up nothing of her own, cellist in a miniskirt, with what a mouth on her against enemies, and a head full of Charles' poems unaltered.

Baltimore

"My lord, he's going to his mother's closet."
—Hamlet

Robert Lowell, a big man, was behind a curtain. The danger of stabbing came from everywhere. A room at Goucher not big enough where my two girlfriends wanted to protect him as the crowd called to more crowds and the crowd cried out for more[1] and the room whined collectively. All the people touched people. Adrienne Rich, his sidekick poet, was happy though suffering from immobility in the crowd as we all were but she was happy in some assumption about the crowd that gave her unwarranted confidence and joy. I know she was glad the two girls persuaded him from out the massive curtains. Now all went well. Now what?

I was only *like* the I who told you. I wanted to fool around with the girls and was afraid of Lowell. Shaking hands was eschewed, there were too many to constantly shake. We were the special students burgeoning though we had no special privileges today and I was not conveniently placed near him. There was no near him there. People woo. The two brave girls reached him through the rabble and spoke delightfully just long enough and so did he, I hate the truth.

The days and their children the years were a boat or they were a river, what do I know? More than likely, compelled by psychological maladjustment or inner strength to a series of actions that led to fireworks. Removed the hostility and aggression of stabbing. Used surprise sparingly. Discussed my fears among themselves. The ache

---

1. Phrase from a song.

to belong, envy of faster guns, flexibility and persistence in poisoning things for others, all eliminated or controlled to the point of metaphor upon which it is not necessary to act. Me, him?

Archive on Ice (After the Act, Pig on the Ice)

In the first matter of Eliot
(There are two)
There was no answer
From a woman named Eliot too,
A perfect form of contempt
One human to another
I've read in *Lingua Franca*
And the *New York Review*
About another matter
(And one had to have lifted from the other).
The poems were rows howed
A second time, green clitorals
Underground severed then.
My guess is *that* (the severed clitorals) was the point
Of the silence, the other wife
's odor in two poems.
Not good, but not bad. She should've let us.
A king needs a drum in back
Each year, and we were.

In the second matter, you can
Look it up almost anywhere
In a four-hundred-page edition,
Dirty rhetoric, clever, nearly
Funny. Not burnt, that's funny.
That's the mystery, like the first four

Pages in my hand, existing.
I guess he thought these were hot
And could inspire or expire
In the Elizabethan sense someone someday.

No one settled for my answers
And we printed nothing.
Maybe he just forgot
In the way you'd leave your genitals
Lying around if they weren't
Attached to your ass
When you start to worry all the time
And smell and that's on your mind.
Shocked at mention of the afterlife,
It says here. That's it then. Good-bye.

This gets curiouser and curiouser
There's a third matter!
In black and white in my file.
Sixty more poems (printed since),
Black lies about female parts
Hidden by him like postcards
Or magazines that are nearly gynecological.

I am keeping all this stuff myself
For the University of Pennsylvania
If they can come up with the cash
And marvelous food at the bash.
I do have the answer to my question,
Which is that we all have something in common,

Even two different kinds of women.
The interesting odor, even today
In my conscious office,
The fish-sweet scent of decay.

Words in Your Mouth

Even a child has old pieces of paper—
Many or just some yellow-stained sheets with notables' or nobles'
Handwriting, as if such a person was only a friend
Without too much power over events or others.
That person has relaxed in a chair and invented a ball game
For the five-year-old who is perhaps in water.
The parents have done something for the person as a person
And he is grateful beyond their wildest dreams
And they are watching, impressed actually with the game.
As I said to my friend Jerry
"It is later the sun will set"
And this is the kind of joke he likes
"And it is still later the sun will rise"
He says. My friend John does not agree
That all of that will stop someday
And there will be no more later.
He says things will be quite different by then,
And this is the kind of joke we like,
Sitting here together, imagining the child,
And supposing the parents at the window behind us.
Do not fear, he says, there will be no end
But the water will not always be blue in front of us,
Or even water and everything will be us.

Gone

Because the moon is too early today
You'd imagine that on the telephone
They'd talk about the typewriter
And on the typewriter (an instrument for one)
They'd talk about the computer
And on the computer they'd talk about the telephone
And on the telephone they'd talk about the piano
And on the piano (an instrument for two)
They'd share the black keys
Never to touch the white! as
They had seen swift burning by the sun
And on the telephone they'd talk about a third
At the piano, the moon like a chipped pearl
Goofy in the blue sky spoke and suggested it
Or perhaps the wisest of the two people, as the wise
Shovel bodies into graves rather than press or force them
Into the dirt, though flowers (or their bulbs)
Are sometimes pressed and pushed there
But best to ease people down into the dirt, cutting the way
With a blade ahead of the body.
While the trigger-happy sun fired at the moon the moon
Suggested the third at the piano be a "student"
They knew, now thirty-eight (this was inappropriate despite her age)
And imagine one switched to only the white
Never to touch the black keys! to
Show it was impossible for three

And imagine they would agree to ask David Shapiro
Who has absorbed all the keys into his feelings
(Called the soul or the musician by various fields)
But actually just the feelings
To finalize the dispute and they would ask him to describe
The musical effect of three at the piano, one hot number
Between the old man and the lewd aging man
Who has suggested some brief sophisticated action
On her part and no return phone call.

The *Iliad*, the *Odyssey*, and *Heart of Darkness*

In fourteen days at sea
The steel ship got very far;
To watch it rip open the waves
While on it was a pleasure per se
And then they closed like water
Closing healed blue on anything.

It got to Greece and did its Odysseus thing
Touring isle by-the-text by isle
Though there had been no such thing or isles
Except in the whim of the great summary
When one placed on a giant veil
Or normal stage curtain the figures passing from the tongue
To the paper, in and out of the threads
People and horses. The people
On the ship knew the point of the books
Was marriage (as when the waves
Opened, closed, and fell, and were waves)
And its trust in the equal adroitness and trust of the other.

Not war.
I have wondered many times if others thought of me.
Remember me, the war song asks, a little
While. I know you won't forget me
But I want you to remember me many times.
How many times did you think of me at sea? Once

Is enough. You are clever at sea.
You are at sea.
Left behind, I am not murdering men here on earth.
An adroitness perfectly balanced between
The woman and the man or else no go Joe.

If we let the transubstantiated figures in on the part
About the return trip by air, the alloys,
The thrust-weight ratio, nothing would fit
And they'd need a nap. We'd give them a map.
They'd think in terms of necessary.
We'd show them everything
And say whose is this?

I wish I wasn't so hard on you.
Somewhere in a tube reading what you do
Or in a jungle captured and tongueless in your car
Or, quite small, in a gunboat speeding afloat in a jar.

THE AUTHOR

ARTHUR VOGELSANG is the author of three previous books of poetry, *A Planet* (Holt, 1983), *Twentieth Century Women* (University of Georgia Press, 1988), and *Cities and Towns* (University of Massachusetts Press, 1996), which received the Juniper Prize. Among anthologies where his work appears are *Best American Poetry, The Pushcart Prize,* and *The New Bread Loaf Anthology.* Since 1973 he has been co-editor of *The American Poetry Review.* He has taught poetry and literature at the University of Iowa, the University of Southern California, and the University of Redlands, and is the recipient of three National Endowment for the Arts fellowships in poetry and a fellowship from the California Arts Council.

Photo by Judith Vogelsang